God Speaks

Devotional Responses to Every 3:16 in the New Testament

By the Members and Friends of the Christian Writers
Fellowship of Western North Carolina (CWF-WNC)

The ministry staff and the congregation of Long's Chapel United Methodist Church are blessed with the presence of the Christian Writers Fellowship on our campus. We are delighted to provide a space for the monthly meetings and to support this wonderful outreach with our prayers. May CWF continue its strong influence beyond the walls of our church through the written word.

—*Reverend Tim McConnell, Long's Chapel UMC*

God Speaks

Devotional Responses to
Every 3:16 in the New Testament

By the Members and Friends of the Christian Writers
Fellowship of Western North Carolina (CWF-WNC)

YAV PUBLICATIONS

ASHEVILLE, NORTH CAROLINA

First Edition

ISBN: 978-1-937449-21-6

Published by:

YAV PUBLICATIONS
ASHEVILLE, NORTH CAROLINA

YAV books may be purchased in bulk
for educational, business, or promotional use.
Contact Books@YAV.com or phone toll-free 888-693-9365.
Visit our website: www.InterestingWriting.com

3 5 7 9 10 8 6 4

Assembled in the United States of America
Published May 2013, Second Printing: December 2013

Abbreviations

Table of Contents

Introduction

One of the most quoted verses in the New Testament is John 3:16—"For God so loved the world that He gave His only begotten Son, that whoever believes in Him should not perish but have everlasting life." (NKJV).

With that one verse embedded in my mind and heart for many years, I became interested in the 3:16s of the other Gospels—Matthew, Mark, and Luke. They also contain basic, but intriguing, truths. I investigated Acts 3:16 and discovered that it, too, was meaningful.

The responses in this book examine the five verses mentioned above as well as the 3:16s in the words written to first-century churches—Romans to Revelation. Twenty-two of those writings are preserved in the New Testament, but only sixteen of them contain a 3:16.

The Christian Writers Fellowship of Western North Carolina (CWF-WNC) invites you to join us as we meditate on these powerful words from the Bible. Nineteen of our members contributed responses to this book. We invite you to add your response on the journal pages that are provided.

As you read, pray for wisdom. Ask God to lead you with His powerful, loving guidance.

Lucy N. Adams, Co-founder
Maureen Miller, Co-founder
Carolyn Underwood, Secretary

Matthew 3:16

When He had been baptized, Jesus came up immediately from the water; and behold, the heavens were opened to Him, and He saw the Spirit of God descending like a dove and alighting upon Him. (NKJV)

Have you ever wondered why Jesus was baptized?

Yes, it is strange because baptism is a response to the forgiveness of sins, and Jesus was the sinless Son of God.

However, He began His ministry by identifying with the people. His cousin, John the Baptist, had been called to start the ministry of Jesus. God, who created the heavens and the earth, as we read in Genesis, was beginning another new creation.

This creation would begin with the birth of Jesus. The heavens that God created "in the beginning" opened when Jesus was baptized. And a dove, which is the symbol of the Spirit, came down to earth. Oh, what a glorious sight it must have been!

God Speaks: My Son Jesus was obedient and saw a magnificent sight.

Prayer: O God, I am blessed with Your plan for baptism and with Your Spirit descending upon me. Amen.

Lucy N. Adams

Matthew 3:16

And when Jesus had been baptized, just as he came up from the water, suddenly the heavens were opened to him and he saw the Spirit of God descending like a dove and alighting on him. (The Jerusalem Bible)

During my devotions one morning, I read that we spend our entire lives growing up into the realization that we are God's beloved. I think how far I have come in my journey of faith and understanding. I know that I still have much to learn. I hunger and thirst to grow closer to God through Jesus Christ—my spiritual compass, heart of my own heart, my best thought.

Jesus' baptism was for Him a revelation from God that brought new certainty and self-understanding of His messianic mission. He was God's Beloved Son and His human life was transformed as His ministry began. A new creation was about to unfold.

In one word, God is love. Scottish theologian George MacDonald said, "The love that foresees creation is itself the power to create." We who live in love and know that we are God's beloved have been shown the source of all that God has intended us to become.

God Speaks: You are My beloved. Live daily in the circle of My love.

Prayer: Dear God, as Your beloved and forgiven child, empower me to be Your new creation. Amen.

Mary Bickerstaff

God Speaks to You

Read Matthew 3:13–17.

What is your response to God's Word today?

_____

_____

_____

_____

_____

_____

_____

_____

_____

_____

_____

_____

_____

What is your prayer today? _____

_____

_____

_____

_____

Mark 3:16

These are the twelve he appointed: Simon (to whom he gave the name Peter). (NIV)

The twelve men who were chosen were special. They were ordinary men, but they were special because they were selected by Jesus! What an honor to be called to walk with Him day by day.

Simon was certainly one of the most vocal. He often expressed his humanness with words of awe. In Matthew 16:16 he said, "Truly you are the Son of God." Simon also promised that he would never deny Jesus even though Jesus knew that His beloved disciple would (Matthew 26:34–35).

That is one of the joys of reading God's Word. Our humanness is seen in those ordinary men. We can identify with some of their positive traits and actions, but also their negative ones.

People have denied Jesus for centuries by refusing to receive Him as their Lord and Savior. Even the Christian who loves and serves Him, sometimes yields to self-will and not God's will.

God Speaks: See yourself in the twelve ordinary men I chose.

Prayer: Thank You, God, that even when I deny You and choose my way, Your love for me is constant and beckons me back. Amen.

Lucy N. Adams

Mark 3:16

And he ordained twelve, that they should be with him, and that he might send them forth to preach, and to have power to heal sicknesses, and to cast out devils: And Simon he surnamed Peter.* (vv.14–16 KJV)

Peter had the attributes he needed for the job he was called to do. He had strength, fortitude, steadiness, firmness of mind, and consistency. We have the qualities God wanted when He called us. Just like Peter, we can do the job God has called us to do.

According to Mark 3:13, Jesus sovereignly chooses "whom he would." He does the choosing. As He told the disciples in John 15:16, "Ye have not chosen me, but I have chosen you, that ye should go and bring forth fruit, and that your fruit should remain: that whatsoever ye shall ask of the Father in my name, he may give it you."

God Speaks: I called you and you responded. I am faithful and responsible. I will guide you and see you through.

Prayer: Lord, thank You for choosing me. I look to You for what I need to fulfill Your purpose in my life. Amen.

Nathan Tracy

*Please read verses 17–19 for the names of the other eleven disciples.

God Speaks to You

Read Mark 3:13–19.

What is your response to God's Word today?

_____

_____

_____

_____

_____

_____

_____

_____

_____

_____

_____

_____

_____

_____

_____

What is your prayer today? _____

_____

_____

_____

_____

Luke 3:16

John answered them all, "I baptize you with water. But one who is more powerful than I will come, the straps of whose sandals I am not worthy to untie. He will baptize you with the Holy Spirit and fire." (NIV)

Who was coming? John the Baptist knew! He knew who Jesus was, why He was more powerful, and why he was not worthy to "untie the thong of His sandals."

John's first encounter with Jesus occurred when Mary, Jesus' mother, visited Elizabeth, John's mother (Luke 1:43–44). He leaped in his own mother's womb when Mary appeared because even then he knew whom Mary carried within her womb.

The water baptism John performed was only a prelude to the baptism of greater power. Jesus would be filled with the Spirit of the Holy God, the Holy Spirit, so that He could fulfill the purpose for which He was sent into the world.

The word *fire* doesn't refer to a real fire. It describes a supernatural event that would occur on the day of Pentecost (Acts 2:3).

God Speaks: All of the words I spoke from the beginning of creation were coming more alive with this event.

Prayer: O God, I am thankful for the birth and obedience of John the Baptist. Help me be obedient, too. Amen.

Lucy N. Adams

Luke 3:16

John answered and said to them all, "As for me, I baptize you with water, but One is coming who is mightier than I, and I am not fit to untie the thong of His sandals. He will baptize you with the Holy Spirit and fire." (NASB)

John the Baptist is proclaiming "*Baruch haba B'Shem Adonai*"—"Blessed is He that comes in the name of the Lord" (Psalm 118:26). He was quick to correct those who thought he was the Messiah promised by the prophets.

During this time period, roads were always dusty and sometimes muddy. Boots and galoshes were unavailable. Household slaves removed the sandals of family members and guests, then bathed their feet. Thus John was characterizing himself as lower than a slave.

Jesus received the anointing of the Holy Spirit for His ministry and the approval of His Father upon His baptism. Those present knew about the Holy Spirit. The Old Testament mentions the Holy Spirit four times and also calls Him the Spirit of God several times. However, no one had yet been baptized in the Holy Spirit; neither was there an understanding of a baptism "in fire."

These baptisms may be seen in several ways. In the first, the believer receives the Holy Spirit during conversion. Secondly, believers also experienced the baptism of the Holy Spirit expressed as "tongues of fire resting on their heads" in Acts 2. That baptism gave the believer bold power to witness and to testify despite persecution. Some believers also received the gift of a prayer language interpreted only by God and by believers gifted with the interpretation of tongues (Acts

2:1–13; 1 Corinthians 12:4–11). Are we not, then, to long for both baptisms and to seek after all God has promised us? May we say with fervor, as John did, "Blessed is He that comes in the name of the LORD" (Psalm 118:26).

God Speaks: I am Lord today, yesterday, and for eternity. My Word holds forever. It is faithful and true.

Prayer: Father God, increase the hunger in my heart to possess every good gift coming down from the Father of Lights. I yearn for everything You have for me! Amen.

Catherine Scott

God Speaks to You

Read Luke 3:15–18.

What is your response to God's Word today?

_____

_____

_____

_____

_____

_____

_____

_____

_____

_____

_____

_____

_____

_____

What is your prayer today? _____

_____

_____

_____

_____

John 3:16

For God loved the world so much that he gave his only Son, so that everyone who believes in him may not die but have eternal life. (TEV)

One autumn afternoon several years ago, I went to the post office to get the mail. As I leafed through my handful of mail, a certain post card sent a cold chill through me.

The letter was addressed to my son, his first notification from a recruiter who was inviting him to enlist in the US Army. I consider myself a patriotic person. In fact, I lived my early childhood on an air base since my dad is a retired Air Force colonel.

But when the remote thought of my son joining the military confronted me, I felt a twinge of panic. *Not my son!* I threw the card in the trash before I even left the post office.

My son never served in the military. He enrolled in college, graduated, and became a scientist. He does research on renewable energy sources.

My heart is filled with gratitude and respect for those who do serve in the military and for their families. When I think of them, I discover I have a more tender heart toward God the Father who gave up His Son to sacrifice His life for me.

God Speaks: I love you so very, very much!

Prayer: God, who loved us before we even had a single thought, help us to understand and appreciate Your gift of grace through Jesus Christ, our Savior and brother. Amen.

Diana Jurss

John 3:16

For God so loved the world, that He gave His only begotten Son, that whoever believes in Him shall not perish, but have everlasting life. (NKJV)

Somehow in today's world, our priorities have become so skewed that what should be first is last and vice versa. Many people, groups, agencies, and companies are demanding loudly and often that we worship the created, rather than the Creator. In fact, some of those folks want to do away with any mention of the Creator at all.

God Almighty, Maker of Heaven and Earth, didn't send His only begotten Son into the world to save polar ice caps, polar bears, tiny rainforest tree frogs, or even the planets. He sent His only begotten Son, Jesus Christ, into the world to save people—you and me—so that we may live with Him here in this life and in the eternal life to come.

That, my friend, is abundantly good news in any age.

God Speaks: Do you know how much I love you?

Prayer: Jesus. Your name says it all. You, Lord, are everything. Forgive me when my attention wavers, my loyalty wanders, and my dedication waffles. It is You I serve, You I love, and You alone who secures my soul. Thank You for the beauty of Your creation. What glorious treasures it holds. You must love us so much, Lord. Thank You, Jesus. You are my life, my reason for being. Jesus. Amen.

Carolyn Underwood

God Speaks to You

Read John 3:1–21.

What is your response to God's Word today?

_____

_____

_____

_____

_____

_____

_____

_____

_____

_____

_____

_____

_____

_____

What is your prayer today? _____

_____

_____

_____

_____

Acts 3:16

And on the basis of faith in His name...Jesus...has given him this perfect health in the presence of you all. (NASB)

The man who received renewed health had been lame from birth. Someone carried him to the gate of the temple each day to beg. His only hope was to receive alms from those who passed by.

What happened when the apostles, Peter and John, passed by is the first healing miracle that is recorded after Pentecost. Even though Peter offered him no money, he asked the beggar to look and to listen. "Silver and gold I do not have, but what I do have I give you: In the name of Jesus Christ of Nazareth, stand up and walk" (Acts 3:6).

The beggar did what Peter commanded. He stood up immediately.

What Jesus had told the disciples was coming true. He had said, "Go into all the world and proclaim the good news to the whole creation" (Mark 16:15). That is what Peter and John had done. They preached. Jesus healed.

The most significant part of this story is that the miracle was performed in the mighty name of Jesus. Paul later wrote, "At the name of Jesus every knee should bend...and every tongue should confess that Jesus Christ is Lord" (Philippians 2:10–11).

God Speaks: Reach out to help others in the mighty name of My Son, Jesus.

Prayer: O God, sometimes I am a beggar who is crippled with sadness or suffering. Thank You for restoration so I can receive healing joy again. Amen.

Lucy N. Adams

Acts 3:16

And his name, through faith in his name, hath made this man strong, whom ye see and know: yea, the faith which is by him hath given him this perfect soundness in the presence of you all. (KJV)

This Scripture gem, nestled within Peter's second sermon, also declares my trust in Him. His name, Jesus, is the foundation of that trust. The name that made strong "this man whom you see and know" intrigues me. Peter states that it's faith in the name that makes one strong.

Early in my life, I had faith in myself, my marriage, and my ability to control my life. I felt strong. Now I'm doing life in prison. That earlier faith proved painfully groundless! Faith in Jesus' name is different. My faith in Him began as "jailhouse religion." "O God," I prayed, "Get me out and I'll…" (fill in the blank). But Jesus didn't leave me there. My faith grew into a wonderful relationship. I not only trust Jesus, I know Him. He's real!

Perfect soundness isn't personal impeccability. Far from it. It's knowing that faith in who Jesus is and what He's done for me transcends everything else in my life. My faith is that Jesus Christ means perfect soundness. And the most amazing thing? Even that faith is given by Him!

God Speaks: Perfect soundness comes only by faith in the name of My Son, Jesus.

Prayer: Dear Lord, please allow me to continue to be an example of Your perfect soundness in the presence of everyone I meet. Amen.

Bruce Wayne Glover

God Speaks to You

Read Acts 3:1–16.

What is your response to God's Word today?

_____

_____

_____

_____

_____

_____

_____

_____

_____

_____

_____

_____

_____

_____

What is your prayer today? _____

_____

_____

_____

_____

Romans 3:16

Their feet are swift to shed blood; ruin and misery mark their ways, and the way of peace they do not know. (vv. 15–17 NIV)

It's tempting to focus on the pronouns in these verses—*their* and *they*—and point the finger at someone else. But if I step back in the passage to Paul's question in verse 9, I recognize that *they* includes *me*.

Paul begins this section of Romans with two questions: "What shall we conclude then? Are we any better?" (v. 9) He's been talking about the difference between Jews and Gentiles, and at this point in his argument, he wants to clarify a significant truth: "As it is written, 'There is none righteous, not even one; there is no one who understands, no one who seeks God'" (vv. 10–11).

I rarely see myself as guilty as others are. Self whispers in my ear, "You're okay." But if I listen to the Holy Spirit, He reminds me that only God is righteous. I am not. The only good in me is the good that flows from God through me.

We're all in the same boat—we're all sinners saved by grace.

God Speaks: Only I can teach you the way of peace. Grace is the doorway; humility, the key that unlocks the door.

Prayer: Good and gracious Father, thank You for forgiving me every time I do wrong. Teach me to see others and myself through Your eyes of grace. Amen.

Denise K. Loock

Romans 3:16

Destruction and misery are in their ways; and the way of peace they have not known. There is no fear of God before their eyes. (vv. 16–18 NKJV)

Lies abound in a world filled with treachery, tolerance, and untruths, a world whose leaders' eyes are not filled with the fear of God but with greed and self-preservation. Truth is morphed into untruth and untruth into falsehood by those who would destroy our nations.

"Where is the truth?" the people ask. "To whom do we turn?" we hear them cry. "Whom do we believe?" echoes in their darkness of unbelief and unknowing.

The answer to all their questions is The One that many people and leaders willfully reject. May the God of Abraham, Isaac, and Jacob have mercy on their souls as He surely does on ours.

God Speaks: Can you hear My warning?

Prayer: Thank You for showing me Your way always and in all ways. Thank You for giving me eyes to see, a heart to believe, and ears to hear. Humility and obedience are difficult for me, Lord. Thank You for Your repeated lessons in the discipline of obedience. Through experiencing You, I've been called to peace, love, life, and mercy. Amen.

Carolyn Underwood

God Speaks to You

Read Romans 3:9–28.

What is your response to God's Word today?

_____

_____

_____

_____

_____

_____

_____

_____

_____

_____

_____

_____

_____

What is your prayer today? _____

_____

_____

_____

_____

1 Corinthians 3:16

Surely you know that you are God's temple, and that God's Spirit lives in you! (TEV)

This simple and direct statement is a powerful clarification of who and what the Holy Spirit is. Many Scriptures have alluded to the presence of God within our inner persons—His breath, His writing on our hearts.

But this verse actually calls us "temples" and says that God's Spirit "dwells" inside each of us. Jesus Himself is the living foundation on which our "temples" are built.

Paul reminds us of the holiness of God's temple and implores us all to live accordingly.

God Speaks: You have a holy houseguest! Keep your temple clean!

Prayer: Heavenly Father, who sends us Your Holy Spirit to live within us, help us to provide clean, peaceful accommodations. Amen.

Diana Jurss

1 Corinthians 3:16

Don't you know you yourselves are God's temple and that God's Spirit lives in you? (NIV)

Of all my household chores, the one I enjoy least is cleaning house. Yet, God has used that chore to teach me how to clean His temple, my body.

One lesson is about the unattended "dust" in His temple. Like the light dust I overlook during daily house cleaning, the light dust of annoyance, fault finding, or a critical mindset seems to be overlooked in His temple as well. I tend to think the light dust isn't an issue since it can't be seen. But when I dust and polish the furniture, I can stand back and see the shine on the wood and smell the sweet aroma of the Murphy's Oil. Likewise, when I clear those negative thoughts, God's glory shines through me and I become His fragrance that appeals to others.

One chore I enjoy is rearranging items to make room for something new. First, I remove everything in that area. Then I begin to discard items I can no longer use. Occasionally, I find items I've misplaced. Sometimes I find things I'd forgotten I had—that's like receiving a gift! The next step is ordering everything. God tells me His temple needs reorganization. Maybe it's overstuffed with unforgiveness, recrimination, or guilt. Those items crowd the space where God's gifts should have been displayed or used.

Sometimes God's temple needs deep cleaning. I need to remove cobwebs of idleness, the dust of idle chatter, and the unpleasant thoughts that have grieved my Father. I also need to let go of those things that are holding me back from being and doing all He desires for me to do and be. And I need to find and use those

God-given gifts that have been hidden, so I can use them for God's glory in building His Kingdom.

God Speaks: Keep My temple clean so that it's a pleasure for Me to live there.

Prayer: Father, how grateful I am to be Your temple. Enable me to continually clean, polish, and rearrange Your temple so others may see Your glory and smell the sweet fragrance of Your Spirit. May that light and sweet aroma draw them to You. Amen.

Erlinda Rogers

God Speaks to You

Read 1 Corinthians 3:12–17.

What is your response to God's Word today?

_____

_____

_____

_____

_____

_____

_____

_____

_____

_____

_____

_____

_____

What is your prayer today? _____

_____

_____

_____

2 Corinthians 3:16

Nevertheless when one turns to the Lord, the veil is taken away. (NKJV)

As a Christian, I've experienced the removal of the veil from my eyes. I know good vision. Seeing clearly now is not only a physical attribute but also a spiritual one—equally necessary to my well-being.

Here's how that happens in my life and perhaps in yours as well: When my eyes are focused on Christ Jesus, nothing else intrudes. However, when I let either my eyes or my thoughts drift ever so slightly, my perception becomes muddled and the Truth veiled. The change is subtle at first, with gauzy grey tones.

Wrongly, I assume that by blinking my eyes I can rid myself of the blurred vision. Perhaps some eye drops. No. What I need at this stage—before it progresses into spiritual blindness—is God's great soul drops. Turning back to the Lord rights my life, restores my sight, and corrects my vision.

God Speaks: I *am* here.

Prayer: Keep me heading in Your direction, Lord. Thank You for correcting my vision in all ways. Amen.

Carolyn Underwood

2 Corinthians 3:16

Whenever, though, they turn to face God as Moses did, God removes the veil and there they are—face-to-face! They suddenly recognize that God is a living, personal presence, not a piece of chiseled stone. (vv. 16–17 MSG)

My family and I used to stroll along the Atlantic City Boardwalk after a day on the beach. What is indelibly imprinted on my mind and heart is a picture of Jesus that was placed in a storefront window. He wore a crown of thorns. When I gazed at His face straight on, it seemed that He was gazing right back at me, looking into the depths of my soul. His eyes were so penetrating that I found it difficult to pull away. If I moved to the right or left, His eyes followed me. When I did manage to move on, I'd turn back to look, and sure enough, His eyes were still following me.

Years later, I experience Jesus as a living, personal presence. He shows me the way to God—the way of Life, Light, and Love. I am irresistibly attracted to Jesus. Through the Risen Christ, I know that God is in me, and I am in God. There's no barrier between us. I can talk to Him about anything, even the darkness.

In the crucifixion of Jesus, God allowed Himself to be temporarily defeated. Out of God's love for His creation, He sent His Son to become one of us. He revealed Himself to the poor, healed the sick, washed feet, celebrated life, and displayed the way of love even when it led to suffering and death.

The resurrection of Jesus Christ was God's great laugh! The veil was lifted. His light shines in our darkness and no darkness can overcome it.

God Speaks: The light I provide can never be extinguished.

Prayer: My God, Your ways are sometimes too much for me to absorb. There's so much I don't understand. Thank You, Jesus, for showing me the way to You. One day I'll see You face to face and become like You. Until then, cover me with Your mercy and grace. Amen.

Mary Bickerstaff

God Speaks to You

Read 2 Corinthians 3:6–18.

What is your response to God's Word today?

_____

_____

_____

_____

_____

_____

_____

_____

_____

_____

_____

_____

_____

_____

What is your prayer today? _____

_____

_____

_____

_____

Galatians 3:16

Now, God made his promises to Abraham and to his descendant. The scripture does not use the plural "descendants," meaning many people, but the singular "descendant," meaning one person only, namely, Christ. (TEV)

This is a very unusual and interesting verse. In the tumultuous time in which we live, many people argue over the Bible's content and meaning. But apparently, even in the early days of the church, when Paul wrote Galatians, there was some hair-splitting discussion over the specific words written in the ancient Scriptures!

Which word was used? Was it past or present tense, singular or plural? What did each word choice imply?

I certainly don't have the answers, but I admit that as a writer I don't always give a lot of thought to my choice of words. I may select one word over another simply because of familiarity.

Perhaps it's not the best use of our time to argue about such minute details. Instead, we should just agree on the most important point: all things in the Bible point to Jesus Christ. He is indeed the lead character.

God Speaks: Everything you need to know can be found in My Son, Jesus Christ.

Prayer: God, who creates and sustains all things, forgive us for our vain and distracted thoughts. Bring our hearts back to completeness in Jesus Christ. Amen.

Diana Jurss

Galatians 3:16

Now the promises were spoken to Abraham and to his seed. He does not say, "And to seeds," as referring to many, but rather to one, "And to your seed," that is, Christ. (NASB)

My husband and I, despite the laws of nature, rebelliously planted a garden in the winter. We planted spinach, radish, several types of lettuce, and zucchini. I even flipped through seed catalogs, deciding which flowers to grow, while snowflakes gathered on the windowsill. We laughed at winter's blustery winds and cold temperatures.

You see, we are blessed with a greenhouse. While it may be 38° outside, the interior of the greenhouse remains a balmy 72°. Light from the sun, even winter's sun, shines down on the exterior, trapping heat inside and warming it beautifully.

Each seed—deposited in the soil, covered, hidden from sight, and then watered with care—eventually sprouted. Then tiny plants stretched upward, bursting with life.

Each seed holds hope. Each one possesses a promise, even though we don't see the fulfillment of our labor immediately. We walk by faith for a season, yes, but the waiting produces joy as we anticipate with gladness the bounty that is certain to come.

As we step into our greenhouse and close the door to winter's chill, we praise the Son from whom all these blessings flow.

God Speaks: Bloom where I planted you.

Prayer: Thank You, kind Father, for Your boundless love and for sending Your precious Son to be the Light of the World and the Living Water. Thank You, that from Abraham's seed, I've inherited the promise of new life through Jesus Christ. Help me as I grow by faith each day. Amen.

Maureen Miller

God Speaks to You

Read Galatians 3:13–24.

What is your response to God's Word today?

_____

_____

_____

_____

_____

_____

_____

_____

_____

_____

_____

_____

_____

_____

What is your prayer today? _____

_____

_____

_____

_____

Ephesians 3:16

I pray that out of his glorious riches he may strengthen you with power through his Spirit in your inner being. (NIV)

My sickness resulted in the need for surgery. It was good to rid myself of the disease, but the result was extreme weakness after the surgery was over. My hope for complete healing grew each day as my body became stronger.

Therefore, I rested and the first place I exercised that hope was within my spirit. Yes, my body was weak, but my spirit and my soul were able to be strong. My body was a mess, but my mind, my emotions, and my will were growing in faith with Jesus' strength.

Praise God this was possible because of His strength in my inner person, which cannot be touched by medicines or surgeries. I have Jesus living in me so that I hear Him say, "My grace is sufficient for you, for My strength is made perfect in weakness" (2 Corinthians 12:9 NKJV).

God Speaks: Never fear. I am here, and I hear your prayers.

Prayer: Loving God, with joy I tell of Your caring touch. I'm thankful that I was temporarily weak in body so that I could better experience Your inner touch of power. Amen.

Lucy N. Adams

Ephesians 3:16

That according to the riches of his glory he may grant you to be strengthened with power through his Spirit in your inner being. (ESV)

The Lord provides foundational strength and character. That gives me abilities of energy, stamina, and discernment. God's power is like the energy source that powers the stars and creates the laws of astrophysics. It continually burns and blazes without being exhausted.

He assures me in Deuteronomy 33:25 that "your strength will equal your days." That assurance of God's inexhaustible power is evident throughout my entire life. The Lord is my strength when His answer is "Yes." He enables me to fulfill His will in my life. The Lord is also my strength when His answer is "No." He provides solace and consolation. He is an omnipresent comfort and provides the hope of heaven's open window as I wait for His will to be revealed. The Lord is my strength when the answer is "Wait." The Holy Spirit says, "Peace. Patience." God's answer will come in His time.

How do I appropriate His strength? I read God's Word until its beauty and truth are sealed in my heart by the interpretation of the Holy Spirit. I pray that my faith and trust in Him will increase in proportion to my needs. As I diminish and as He increases, His power replaces my weakness and is perfected in me. How wonderful to walk in the divine power of the Creator of the Universe.

God Speaks: Rely on Me, dear child of My heart, until you look to Me for your every breath.

Prayer: Father God, please increase my reliance upon You and my faith in Your strength. Amen.

Catherine Scott

God Speaks to You

Read Ephesians 3:14–20.

What is your response to God's Word today?

_____

_____

_____

_____

_____

_____

_____

_____

_____

_____

_____

_____

_____

_____

What is your prayer today? _____

_____

_____

_____

Philippians 3:16

However that may be, let us go forward according to the same rules we have followed until now. (TEV)

Whenever we ponder select verses of the Bible, we need to be mindful of their historical context. In this instance, Paul is writing a letter to the first church he established on European soil. He was apparently stressed because some false teaching had crept into the church at Philippi.

Philippians 3:16 reminds us that no matter how wise, sophisticated, educated, or powerful we become, we need to always remain faithful to the basic truths of Christianity—namely, Jesus Christ! Paul goes on to say that spiritually mature Christians need to set a good example, and he emphasizes that we are not afforded special privileges superior to those who are new in the faith.

What a great message indeed! We are all made equal through Jesus Christ, a very new and radical thought to those who lived in Paul's era.

God Speaks: I, the Truth, do not change.

Prayer: Lord, we praise You for keeping things simple for us. You are King and Your kingdom endures forever. Amen.

Diana Jurss

Philippians 3:16

Only let our conduct fit the level we have already reached.
(CJB)

The church at Philippi was facing strong opposition from members who still clung to things of the world. Paul appears to be concerned that others might backslide and rediscover purpose in legalism. He tells the church to "pursue the goal in order to win the prize offered by God's upward calling in the Messiah Jesus" (3:14 CJB).

Paul states that if confidence in human qualifications hits the mark, then he should have won the righteousness lottery. But he has relinquished his prior legalistic beliefs in exchange for the value of knowing Jesus as Lord and receiving faith-based righteousness from God. He counsels the Philippians to draw strength from unifying in common purpose and love, in heart and in mind with the Lord.

Winning or "attaining the goal" is a process. A change of heart results in attitudinal change, followed by behavioral change. Those changes evidence the believer's commitment to the transforming work of the Holy Spirit. The process builds upon its own attainments and ever strains upward toward Jesus, the author and finisher of our faith (Hebrews 12:2).

Paul asks the church members to demonstrate the power of the Lord's transformation in their actions. That is the test of our witness: Can people be won to Jesus Christ without a word?

God Speaks: Hold tightly to Me. I will not let your foot slip. I, who watch over you, will not slumber (Psalm 121:3 paraphrased).

Prayer: Father God, may I be found faithful in You. May my progress in You move forward and reflect Your glory. Amen.

Catherine Scott

God Speaks to You

Read Philippians 3:15–21.

What is your response to God's Word today?

_____

_____

_____

_____

_____

_____

_____

_____

_____

_____

_____

_____

_____

_____

What is your prayer today? _____

_____

_____

_____

_____

Colossians 3:16

Let the word of Christ dwell in you richly in all wisdom, teaching and admonishing one another in psalms and hymns and spiritual songs, singing with grace in your hearts to the Lord. (NKJV)

Many years ago the Book of Psalms was the hymnbook of the temple. We sing today from that same sacred book and also from thousands of hymns that inspired composers wrote. When we accept Jesus Christ as our Savior, there is a newness in singing, for God puts a new song in our mouths (Psalm 40:3).

Moses and the Israelites sang in thanksgiving to God after Pharaoh's army was destroyed in the Red Sea (Exodus 15:1–18). And Jesus sang! Matthew 26:30 says, "When they had sung a hymn, they went out to the Mount of Olives."

If I cannot sleep at night, I resist my tendency to fret, and I sing within myself. My mouth is closed and my eyes are closed, but I am open to worship as I fall back into a peaceful sleep.

God Speaks: When I created all things, I made birds to sing. Listen to their music.

Prayer: Thank You, O God, for the deep need I have to hear Your music. It touches my soul and can bring You glory! Amen.

Lucy N. Adams

Colossians 3:16

Let the word of Christ dwell in you richly in all wisdom, teaching and admonishing one another in psalms and hymns and spiritual songs, singing with grace in your hearts to the Lord. (NKJV)

God was so good not to waste a singing voice on me on this earth. I love music. I love lyrics. I love rhythm and praising Jesus in song. Music restores and elevates my soul.

So why would a singing voice be wasted on me? Music that glorifies my Lord makes me cry. It's impossible to sing well and cry at the same time. For those like me, who are tunefully challenged, crying absolutely nullifies singing. And singing on key? Forget that! So for now I am resigned to "singing with grace in my heart to the Lord."

Even if you suffer through my correct-note-challenged voice here on earth, there's hope. I've no doubt that God is going to let me praise Him with a knock-you-back-on-your-heels bodacious voice when I arrive in my heavenly home. Just you wait and hear.

God Speaks: The Christ factor, from the inside out, is everything.

Prayer: O generous God, lover of our souls, giver of gifts divine, thank You for gifting me with personal pitch. What an honor it is to have a singing voice that only You could love. I love you! Amen.

Carolyn Underwood

God Speaks to You

Read Colossians 3:15–17.

What is your response to God's Word today?

_____

_____

_____

_____

_____

_____

_____

_____

_____

_____

_____

_____

_____

_____

What is your prayer today? _____

_____

_____

_____

_____

2 Thessalonians 3:16

Now may the Lord of peace Himself give you peace always in every way. The Lord be with you all. (NKJV)

Who wants peace? I do, you do, we all do. The alternative of peace is anguish, fear, and frustration. No one desires that. But since the Lord of peace gives it, my relationship with Him must be solid for me to experience peace. My faith in the promise of peace is essential.

Jesus assured the disciples, "Peace I leave with you, my peace I give you. I do not give as the world gives" (John 14:27 NIV). So often my happiness comes from the world, but it can only provide external pleasures for a short time. They do not satisfy and they lead to anguish.

God Speaks: Do you listen to the chatter of the world more often than you listen to Me? That might be a trap that keeps you from hearing My words of peace.

Prayer: O God of peace, I need Your kind of peace. Thank You for making that possible. Amen.

Lucy N. Adams

2 Thessalonians 3:16

May the Lord himself, who is our source of peace, give you peace at all times and in every way. The Lord be with you all (TEV)

Paul closes his second letter to the Thessalonians with this short but profound prayer. He had admonished them quite sharply in the previous paragraphs for being lazy! He accused some of them of not working and of accepting financial support that they hadn't earned. He told them they should live orderly lives, earn their own living, and not take advantage of others.

Paul then prays for the Lord to grant them peace. Such a valuable gift! A peaceful mind is a fruitful place where good things can grow—unlike a lazy mind that produces selfishness and strife. The peace that comes from God brings a holiness to all situations.

This prayer is one we can pray over our friends in every circumstance.

God Speaks: Ask Me to reveal to you how accessible My peace is.

Prayer: Oh Lord, we make life so much more difficult and complicated than it needs to be. The slightest glimpse of Your love for us provides a bounty of peace. Amen.

Diana Jurss

God Speaks to You

Read 2 Thessalonians 3:11–16.

What is your response to God's Word today?

_____

_____

_____

_____

_____

_____

_____

_____

_____

_____

_____

_____

_____

_____

What is your prayer today? _____

_____

_____

_____

1 Timothy 3:16

And without controversy great is the mystery of godliness: God was manifested in the flesh, justified in the Spirit, seen by the angels, preached among the Gentiles, believed on in the world, received up in glory. (NKJV)

Let's solve the mystery! Paul does it in an exciting way. By using other parts of Scripture, the six descriptions of godliness are explained. Jesus came to the world in a body—baby Jesus. He was justified—made right—in the Spirit (John 1:14); He was seen by angels (Matthew 28:2). He was preached among the Gentiles (Romans 10:18), believed on in the world (Colossians 1:6, 23), and taken up into glory (Luke 21:51).

There's no excuse for not understanding the full story of God's plan. He has clearly stated it in His Word. Hallelujah!

God Speaks: Those who are disciples of Jesus are forever united in My Word.

Prayer: Thank You, Jesus, for fulfilling all the prophecies—for living among us and dying for us, and for Your glorious resurrection. Amen.

Lucy N. Adams

1 Timothy 3:16

Beyond all question, the mystery of godliness is great: He appeared in a body, was vindicated by the Spirit, was seen by angels, was preached among the nations, was believed on in the world, and was taken up in glory. (NIV)

Paul wrote these words to Timothy. Formerly, Paul had been Saul, a man of violence known to "breathe out murderous threats against Jesus Christ's followers" (Acts 9:1). He was willing to travel great distances to capture them so they could be put to death.

One day, when Saul was traveling to Damascus, a bright light came from heaven and a voice questioned, "Saul, Saul, why do you persecute me?"

He immediately answered, "Who are you, Lord?"

Saul knew who was speaking to him, but he did not personally know Jesus Christ. Blinded, he obeyed, went into the city, and was taught many things by Jesus Christ's followers, the very ones he had intended to arrest.

This verse in Scripture could be considered Paul's confession that beyond anyone's questions, Christ Jesus was the long awaited Messiah. Timothy knew about Paul's breathtaking conversion. Since Paul had faith in Timothy's potential leadership and was aware he would encounter many ministerial and relational problems in the early churches, he offered these words of assurance.

God Speaks: Beyond all question, Jesus Christ is the Messiah.

Prayer: Our Father, we thank You for allowing us to benefit from the Word that You graciously have given us because it gives us a glimpse into Your greatness. We pray that the Holy Spirit will work in us and that we will be a testimony for You. Amen.

Dee Shaw

God Speaks to You

Read 1 Timothy 3:14–16.

What is your response to God's Word today?

_____

_____

_____

_____

_____

_____

_____

_____

_____

_____

_____

_____

_____

What is your prayer today? _____

_____

_____

_____

_____

2 Timothy 3:16

All Scripture is inspired by God and is useful for teaching the truth, rebuking error, correcting faults, and giving instructions for right living. (TEV)

This well-known and oft quoted verse comes from Paul's second letter to his young colleague and dear friend, Timothy. What I find so lovely and providential is that Paul probably had no idea that what he was writing would also eventually become Scripture!

The Scripture to which he referred in this verse was surely the ancient Jewish texts. Paul just thought he was writing a helpful letter of advice and encouragement to an aspiring pastor.

But our wonderful God is gracious enough to work through us flawed human beings, to allow us to participate in His grand scheme of blessing. We are not only members of His kingdom, but also we are actually allowed to help raise it up. Every time we write a note of encouragement to somebody, we too are building up God's people.

God Speaks: Dear children, the Bible is so much more than just a good book.

Prayer: Divine writer and orator, creator of all words, languages, and thought patterns, thank You for thinking of us. Thank You for revealing Yourself to us in ways we can comprehend. Amen.

Diana Jurss

2 Timothy 3:16

All Scripture is God-breathed and is useful for teaching, reproof, correcting and training in righteousness. (ISV)

On February 26, 1999, I discovered that the Bible is true and that every word in it came from God Himself. I came to this knowledge in my late forties, not because I had read 2 Timothy 3:16—I hadn't even read John 3:16 yet. Rather, I discovered it in the minutes following a life-changing encounter with Jesus.

In the weeks and months that followed that brief but profound encounter with our Lord, I studied everything I could find about Him and His Book. I installed myself in the chair next to the shelf of English-language books at the Christian bookstore in Haarlem, The Netherlands. The proprietor, Job (pronounced "Jope, like "hope," in Dutch), befriended me. He understood more about what was happening to me than I did.

I soon memorized John 3:16. Shortly after that, I read 2 Timothy 3:16, which confirmed what I had known since that life-changing day in February: The Bible is a work of non-fiction!

Yes, 2 Timothy 3:16 is one of the most important Bible verses for me because it assures me that other verses, which provide guidance for my life, are true: Matthew 6:33, 1 Corinthians 10:13, Philippians 4:13, John 11:25, and John 14:6. Another Biblical truth that undergirds my life is Jeremiah 31:17: "'So there is hope for your future,' declares the LORD."

God Speaks: The Bible is true, every word of it.

Prayer: Thank You, Lord, for giving us Your Word, unchanging and ever true. Please preserve and protect my faith in You. Keep it unwavering and ever pure. Amen.

Chris Yavelow

God Speaks to You

Read 2 Timothy 3:14–17.

What is your response to God's Word today?

_____

_____

_____

_____

_____

_____

_____

_____

_____

_____

_____

_____

_____

_____

What is your prayer today? _____

_____

_____

_____

_____

Hebrews 3:16

For who, having heard, rebelled? Indeed, was it not all who came out of Egypt, led by Moses? (NKJV)

I felt as if I had been thrown into the wilderness when my husband wanted a divorce. Since it was not my choice, I became rebellious and very angry. During the next year, I studied God's Word more diligently than I ever had.

If we look back to Hebrews 3:15, we see the whole picture—"Today, if you will hear His voice, do not harden your hearts as in the rebellion." As I meditated on God's Word, I recognized my lack of faith and rebellion in my marriage. I had become hard-hearted, and I complained about everything when I did not get my way.

Now I believe that listening to God is the first requirement of walking by faith. If we do not depend on Him, we begin to walk in the wrong direction. God will test us, just as He tested the Israelites in the wilderness. He desires that we learn from our failures. The first step is acknowledging them and repenting.

God Speaks: If you want to walk in the right direction, you must follow My instructions.

Prayer: Loving Father, soften my heart so that I desire to obey Your Word. Amen.

Gerry Burke

Hebrews 3:16

For who provoked Him when they had heard? Indeed, did not all those who came out of Egypt led by Moses? (NASB)

To provoke someone is to arouse in them a strong displeasure, usually in response to unjust or offensive behavior. The writer of Hebrews is referring to the Israelites who had witnessed the parting of the Red Sea and heard God speak at Mt. Sinai, yet they refused to enter the Promised Land when they arrived at Kadesh-Barnea (Numbers 14:1–3).

Their rebellious unbelief provoked God. He had delivered them from Pharaoh, provided food and water in the desert, and established an everlasting covenant with them. But they decided that He couldn't triumph over the giants in Canaan. So they said to Moses, "Let's go back to Egypt."

Shamelessly disrespectful, right? And yet, I also sometimes respond to God's promises with insolent unbelief: "How will I restore peace in my family?" "What will I do about all these unpaid bills?" "Who will steer my wayward teenager back to God?"

Sometimes we're tempted to "go back to Egypt"— to rely on our culture's solutions or our own schemes instead of God's promises. That's when we need a good dose of Caleb-and-Joshua faith. They stood together against two million naysayers and declared, "The LORD is with us: don't be afraid" (Numbers 14:9).

God Speaks: Rely on Me and bring Me joy. I am utterly trustworthy.

Prayer: Gracious God, when I'm tempted to doubt You, remind me of Your faithfulness. Amen.

Denise K. Loock

God Speaks to You

Read Hebrews 3:12–19.

What is your response to God's Word today?

_____

_____

_____

_____

_____

_____

_____

_____

_____

_____

_____

_____

_____

_____

_____

What is your prayer today? _____

_____

_____

_____

_____

James 3:16

For where envying and strife is, there is confusion and every evil work. (KJV)

Nobody wants to be called a fool; we would all like to be considered wise. But how can we grow wisdom instead of foolishness in our hearts?

As Proverbs is the Old Testament book of wisdom, James is the New Testament book of wisdom. Envy and strife, James says, are the fruit of earthly wisdom. Envy demands, "I deserve more—prestige, possessions, power." Strife says, "I'll do whatever it takes to get more, no matter whom I trample." Envy asks, "How can God be good if He's not giving me what I desire?" Strife suggests, "God must not be powerful enough to provide what I want, so I'll get it myself." James says that kind of foolish, self-absorbed thinking is destructive.

On the other hand, a humble, others-centered attitude is characteristic of heavenly wisdom. Believing that God will provide for me regardless of what others have or what others do is a sign that I'm relying on His goodness and power. That mindset produces peace-making, gentleness, mercy, and sincerity in my life (v. 17).

Am I cultivating wisdom or foolishness in my heart?

God Speaks: If you want to be wise, uproot selfishness and cultivate My truth in your heart.

Prayer: All-Wise God, help me to discard the selfish desires that produce envy and strife. Plant gentleness and mercy in my heart. Amen.

Denise K. Loock

James 3:16

For where jealousy and selfish ambition exist, there is disorder and every evil thing. (NASB)

As a woman of eighty-eight years, I remember WWII. In 1943, the Allies were losing disastrously. A junior in college, I was frightened of a possible loss. I fantasized about being arrested because I was a Christian and being placed in solitary confinement. I memorized Scripture, just in case, so my mind would have something to think about to keep from going insane.

James 3:16 was a verse I had read only casually, but as a child I had learned the Ten Commandments. Number Ten is "Thou shalt not covet." Other references to jealousy are scattered throughout the Bible. Jealousy may not seem as important as other sins, but God looks on the heart and knows our every sinful thought. And jealousy can lead to other sins: it can cause rage intense enough to kill, envy potent enough to steal, or lust passionate enough to commit adultery.

James explains how we can avoid jealousy: God's wisdom is peace-loving and courteous. It allows discussion and willingly yields to others; it's full of mercy and good deeds. It is wholehearted, straightforward, and sincere.

God Speaks: If you allow Me to fill your heart with peace, there'll be no room for jealousy.

Prayer: Cleanse my heart of jealousy and selfish ambition, O God, so that I might promote peace in my sphere of influence and keep my heart pure. Amen.

Helen Hughes Rice

God Speaks to You

Read James 3:13–18.

What is your response to God's Word today?

_____

_____

_____

_____

_____

_____

_____

_____

_____

_____

_____

_____

_____

_____

What is your prayer today? _____

_____

_____

_____

_____

1 Peter 3:16

Do what is right; then if men speak against you, calling you evil names, they will become ashamed of themselves for falsely accusing you when you have only done what is good. (TLB)

"I just want to do what's right!" For as long as I can remember those words have been one of my brother's favorite phrases. Whether it has to do with a decision on playing a family game, going out to eat (barbecue or fish), or making a major decision on a group vacation, his response invariably is, "I just want to do what's right."

Imagine my surprise when I found that statement in 1 Peter 3:16 in the paraphrased Living Bible: "Do what is right." Earlier verses in chapter 3 focus on living in harmony, loving, being compassionate and humble, and refusing to repay evil with evil.

Sometimes Christians aren't as active in the pursuit of peace as we should be. How often do we avoid someone who has hurt our feelings or treated us badly? On the other hand, how often have we failed to seek compromise or refused to see another's point of view?

Jesus Christ died in our place, for our sins. The most holy and righteous person who ever lived, who only did what was good, sacrificed His life that we might live with Him eternally. Surely, following the example of Jesus Christ in seeking to "do what is right" is a worthy goal for all of us.

I think my brother has the right idea in striving to be a person who always wants to do what's right. Perhaps I should go and do likewise.

God Speaks: Doing and acting right with gentleness and respect in all circumstances gives you an opportunity to show My love to all people.

Prayer: Dear Father, You are holy and only do what is right for Your people. Help us to seek righteousness, to do what is right in all situations. Amen.

Mary Jo Maples

1 Peter 3:16

Keeping a clear conscience, so that those who speak maliciously against your good behavior in Christ may be ashamed of their slander. (NIV)

Talk is cheap. Proof is free.

Jesus told us to be living testimonies of God's power. The best and quickest way to settle a dispute is to live it out through actions that others are unable to refute. Living a life that displays God's power does far more to prove He is real than any persuasive argument.

Scripture tells us that we get to God by following Jesus. Following Him is taking the road less traveled. Once we pass through "the narrow gate," we travel a different path (Matthew 7:13–14). We refuse to go *with* the flow, and sometimes we're compelled to go *against* it. We reason differently and respond differently than others do—the living proof of Jesus in us.

Peter warns us that, like Jesus, we may be ridiculed and rejected. But then he gives us hope: if Jesus is our Lord, we don't need the world's approval. We have nothing to fear. We're far better off with the Lord's blessing for doing what is right.

God's power at work in us produces the fruit of the Spirit and sets us apart (Galatians 5:22–23). When others notice that we're different, we should credit Jesus as the reason. When words alone are not enough to justify us, His Spirit shining through us will prove our case. We defend ourselves against the world's ridicule by living lives of integrity.

When the world mocks our behavior, we don't have to argue to defend ourselves. If we speak the truth in gentleness and humility, our character will prove us right.

God Speaks: Don't worry about defending yourself. I'll protect My name and I'll protect You.

Prayer: Lord, show Yourself to the world through me. I offer my life as a platform for Your power. Give me the strength and humility to follow Jesus all the way and the courage to accept the world's ridicule in exchange for Your blessing. Amen.

Beth Pleming

God Speaks to You

Read 1 Peter 3:13–17.

What is your response to God's Word today?

_____

_____

_____

_____

_____

_____

_____

_____

_____

_____

_____

_____

_____

What is your prayer today? _____

_____

_____

_____

_____

2 Peter 3:16

Also in all his [Paul's] epistles, speaking in them of these things, in which are some things hard to understand, which untaught and unstable people twist to their own destruction, as they do also the rest of the Scriptures. (NKJV)

Peter directed this biting verse to the false teachers of his day. If we put the verse into modern context, who would be the "unstable" and "untaught" people that fail to understand and twist the Scriptures to their own destruction? At one time I thought I knew who they were: high school teachers, college professors, work associates, some friends, lots of Christians, and even pew mates from church. Those folks couldn't teach me much about the Bible. In their ignorance they were surely blazing a path to their own destruction. Yes, Lord, I felt comfortable identifying them…but should I have been?

Ironically, as my relationship with Jesus Christ matured, scriptural meanings I thought were clear became a little harder to understand. Had I misinterpreted or misunderstood their meaning? Yes, often. Had I been overly vocal and pushy in expressing my views? Yes, definitely. Had I been so stone cold sure of some Biblical matter that I couldn't or wouldn't entertain an objective counterpoint or discussion? Yes, that too. Maybe I should have listened more closely to what those I had identified as ignorant—thus doomed—had said about the Christian faith.

In fact, I was the one who was untaught and unstable in my understanding of the Scriptures. Two thousand years ago, Peter was speaking to me. I'm thankful that Jesus Christ transformed my understanding of God's Holy Word and my life.

God Speaks: Be worthy in your understanding of My Word.

Prayer: Heavenly Father, thank You for giving me the patience and ability to learn and grow in my understanding of Your Holy Word through Scripture and through my Christian brothers and sisters. I praise You for transforming my life through Your Son, Jesus Christ our Lord, Savior, and Friend, in whose name I pray. Amen.

Ron Miller

2 Peter 3:16

He writes the same way in all his letters, speaking in them of these matters. His letters contain some things that are hard to understand, which ignorant and unstable people distort, as they do the other Scriptures, to their own destruction. (NIV)

Peter wrote about the last days to build confidence in Jesus Christ's return. With an emphasis on holy living, he urges us to pursue godliness so that we'll be ready.

Peter also warns that critics will mock us. Yet we are to wait patiently and expectantly, trusting God's Word. We stand firm knowing His Word is powerful and trustworthy, that by His voice alone the earth was created and destroyed. We strive for holiness because we trust that Jesus Christ's return will bring punishment and rewards, the creation of a new heaven and earth.

Even if God's timing seems slow, we shouldn't lose hope. What seems slow to humans is a fleeting moment on God's timetable. God has good reason for the delay—He wants everyone to come to repentance. Though Jesus Christ's return may seem distant, we are to live as though it is imminent.

Peter ends his letter by saying, "Don't just take my word for it. Paul preached the same message, inspired by divine wisdom" (vv. 15–16, author paraphrase). We shouldn't be discouraged if Paul's teaching seems difficult to grasp. Peter struggled to understand it also. Ignorant people who don't know any better will twist the meaning of Scripture to fit their own understanding, but we rely on God to bring insight through revelation as we seek Him for truth.

God Speaks: I *am* coming. Be patient.

Prayer: Lord, give me wisdom and discernment to know Truth, courage to stand on Your Word, patience to trust in Your timing, and strength to live a life that is holy while I wait patiently for Your return. Amen.

Beth Pleming

God Speaks to You

Read 2 Peter 3:10-18.

What is your response to God's Word today?

_____

_____

_____

_____

_____

_____

_____

_____

_____

_____

_____

_____

What is your prayer today? _____

_____

_____

_____

_____

1 John 3:16

This is how we know what love is: Jesus Christ laid down his life for us. And we ought to lay down our lives for our brothers. (NIV)

We can know through the world's greatest Lover what true love is. Jesus was there at the beginning with God, the awesome Creator of the entire universe. Jesus spoke the world into existence with affirmation, joy, excitement, and the sincerity of His love for mankind.

"The Word became flesh and dwelt among us" (John 1:14 KJV). Jesus Christ put love into action every day of His life. He healed the sick, gave sight to the blind, and told the paralytic to take up his bed and walk (Mark 2:9). Jesus spoke words of forgiveness and encouragement; He visited the homes of the hated and loved them all in spite of their sin. The first twelve disciples lived with and witnessed this Person called both God and Man—the Man, Christ Jesus. They felt His touch of love and heard His words, "You're forgiven." In addition, they saw Him willingly lay down His life in death for the sins of the entire world.

In this new life of love and abandonment to Jesus, we are to recognize the responsibility, the command, and then the privilege to "lay down"—to give ourselves in self-sacrifice—for our brothers and sisters in Jesus.

God Speaks: Living in love speaks louder than our words.

Prayer: Dear Heavenly Father and Creator of the Universe, we praise Your Holy Name. Thank You for revealing Your loving nature through Your self-sacrificing Son, Jesus Christ our Savior. Amen.

Shelia Berry

1 John 3:16

This is how we know what love is: Jesus Christ laid down his life for us. And we ought to lay down our lives for our brothers. (NIV)

God commanded us to do two things above all else: believe in the name of His Son Jesus, and love our neighbors. Love is one of the most frequently mentioned topics in Scripture—a theme woven into every story.

Love isn't just something we say or an emotion we feel. Love is something we *do*. Just as Jesus laid down His life in a literal, physical sense, we're called to lay down our lives by putting others before ourselves.

The stakes are high. Jesus said other people will recognize us as God's children by the way we love them (John 13:35). Loving others the way Jesus loves us demonstrates our uniqueness. It's our trademark.

The world tells us to love those who love us back and to stop loving people who don't return the favor; to help others when it doesn't cost us too much; to do for others *along* the way without going *out* of our way; to take care of ourselves first and look out for others with what's left over.

But Jesus gave sacrificially with no strings attached even when it wasn't reciprocated. He gave extravagantly—without limits—although it cost Him everything. He loved both those who loved Him back and those who hated Him. He continues to love even when He receives little, if any, love in return.

Jesus gave His life as the ultimate love sacrifice, but He also spent His earthly life loving people in practical ways—caring for the sick, providing for the poor, healing the wounded, praying for the lost, and serving

His companions. Love wasn't just something He talked about; it was something He *did*.

God Speaks: I am your Role Model. That's how you know what love is.

Prayer: Lord, thank You for the sacrifice You made to show me what love is, for Your unfailing love that knows no limits. Give me a heart that loves like Yours does. Teach me how to love others well and sacrificially, with humility and perseverance. Amen.

Beth Pleming

God Speaks to You

Read 1 John 3:13–16.

What is your response to God's Word today?

_____

_____

_____

_____

_____

_____

_____

_____

_____

_____

_____

_____

_____

_____

What is your prayer today? _____

_____

_____

_____

_____

Revelation 3:16

I know your deeds, that you are neither cold nor hot. I wish you were either one or the other! So because you are lukewarm—neither hot nor cold—I am about to spit you out of my mouth. (vv. 15–16 NIV)

Like all human beings, my greatest weakness has been my sinful nature that separates me from God. Though I didn't have to be saved from sins such as murder, drunkenness, drug addiction, or adultery (what we often call "the big sins"), I had to admit to and ask forgiveness for one sin (among many others) that may be the most serious sin of all. I had constantly been committing the sin of lukewarmness.

I like food either hot or cold. Lukewarm food is not only less tasteful, but it also spoils much more easily. Similarly, God has said that He doesn't want lukewarm followers; they nauseate Him.

This doesn't mean that we need to be constantly preaching at others, but it does mean we should be continually serving them like Jesus did. Our apathy and timidity in sharing our faith, particularly in our workplace, manifest our lukewarm tendencies.

God Speaks: Everyone's a sinner. No one's sins are more or less offensive to Me than anyone else's. I'm willing and eager to forgive them all. Just ask.

Prayer: Lord, forgive me for being lukewarm. Please light a fire within me. Amen.

Bernard L. Brown, Jr.

Revelation 3:16

So, because you are lukewarm and neither cold nor hot, I will spew you out of My mouth! (AMP)

I love this verse. It encourages my passion for God and boosts my soul when I feel overcome by the sin in this world and underwhelmed by the mediocrity that pervades our culture.

God doesn't call us to be fence-sitting followers with no impact in the world. He calls us to be on fire for Him, eagerly urging others to know Him, the God of miracles and might. He calls us to be water-walkers, disciples who follow Him 100 percent, willing to do what He says to do and to go where He says to go.

When was the last time you took a lukewarm shower? If it's been a while, do it. Within seconds you'll be warming up the water perhaps so much that you'll then turn it in the opposite direction to cool down. Not anything that is lukewarm is appealing: not the food we eat, the drinks we consume, or the water in which we bathe. Why on earth would we tolerate it in the most important relationship in our lives? God doesn't.

God Speaks: Do you know what makes Me sad to the point of vomiting?

Prayer: Lord, forgive my wishy-washy ways with You. Turn me on, heat me up, and set me loose for You in this lukewarm world. In Jesus' name, amen.

Carolyn Underwood

God Speaks to You

Read Revelation 3:14–22.

What is your response to God's Word today?

_____

_____

_____

_____

_____

_____

_____

_____

_____

_____

_____

_____

_____

_____

_____

What is your prayer today? _____

_____

_____

_____

Acknowledgments

Special thanks to the following:

Our Lord and Savior Jesus Christ whose guidance we seek.

Long's Chapel United Methodist Church for reserving a meeting place for our Christian Writers Fellowship of Western North Carolina (CWF-WNC) each month since our first meeting in January 2009.

The Prayer Ministry of Long's Chapel UMC for their financial gift toward the publication of *God Speaks*.

The Agape Link of the United Methodist Women for their financial gift.

Kathi Macias, author of over forty books, friend and special guest at one of our first meetings. To help raise money for the publication of *God Speaks*, she donated ten copies of her best seller, *Unexpected Christmas Hero*, to the CWF-WNC.

Foundation for Evangelism at Lake Junaluska, NC, for their generous gift of Bibles, *The Faith Sharing New Testament with Psalms*.

Disciple Bible Outreach Ministries of Western North Carolina for their financial gift toward the publication of *God Speaks*.

Jim Starnes (1936–2013) for his membership in the CWF-WNC from its inception until his death. With his wife, Myrtle, he contributed his writing skills and his faithful Christian commitment to our Lord.

Chris Yavelow who joined our Christian Writers Fellowship in January 2011. He has faithfully shared with us his gifts of writing and publishing. We are thankful that one of our own members published *God Speaks*.

Denise Loock, editor, who graciously organized the Scriptures, prayers, and responses and then created a cohesive manuscript.

Members of the CWF-WNC who contribute their time, skills, and prayers for each other at our meetings. Many of them also contributed financial gifts toward the publication of *God Speaks*.

About the Contributors

Lucy Neeley Adams loves to write and tell stories. She is the author of *52 Hymn Story Devotions* (www.52hymns.com), and she is a columnist for several newspapers. She has written for Crosswalk.com and The Upper Room, and she has contributed stories for several books. Since she is one of the co-founders of CWF-WNC, this 3:16 project, with contributions from members, is a dream come true. She and her husband, Woody, live at Lake Junaluska, North Carolina. Drop her a line at lucya424@aol.com.

Shelia Berry, writer, speaker, and graduate of William Carey University in Hattiesburg, Mississippi, is the mother of three children and Nana of two precious granddaughters. She enjoys reading the Bible mainly but also other types of books. Other joys include journaling, writing devotions, walking, and spending time with family and friends.

Mary Bickerstaff has enjoyed poetry, prose, and fiction as long as she can remember. She gleans messages of hope and healing from her lengthy career in the medical profession and incorporates them in her writing. She completed a two-year course with the Institute of Children's Literature and has been published in *Pockets Magazine* and Devo Kids. Currently, she's working on a book that chronicles her battle with Stage 1 breast cancer. Bickerstaff is a CWF-WNC charter member.

Bernie Brown, a preacher's kid, retired as the CEO of one of the largest non-profit healthcare systems in the country. As a "refiree," he volunteers, writes, teaches, speaks, consults, and mentors. He is a Christian and active in his church. Bernie has been married to Snookie for fifty years, and they have three children and six grandchildren. They reside in Marietta, Georgia, and Lake Junaluska, North Carolina.

Gerry Burke was born in Tulsa, Oklahoma. She's been a resident of North Carolina for twenty-six years and has lived in Waynesville for the past fifteen years. A pastor who was a visiting evangelist for an Ashram at Lake Junaluska, North Carolina, encouraged her to write when he heard her testimony. Being a member of the Christian Writers Fellowship has been a great encouragement.

Bruce Wayne Glover was raised in Sebring, Florida, with his older brother, Norman Timothy. Glover has written for various magazines. One of his devotions, published in *The Upper Room* in 2010, is a strong witness to the power of Jesus Christ in his life. When he heard about the publication of this book, he asked if he could send a response to Acts 3:16, which we happily received.

Diana Jurss was raised in Indiana and graduated from Purdue University. She and her husband live in a small town in Western North Carolina and have two grown children. She's been writing poetry since she was a child and has studied under several gifted poets. Her work has appeared in numerous small presses including the *Asheville Poetry Review*. She is a pharmacist employed by a rural hospital. A book of her poetry, *An Alphabet of Sixty-Six Letters*, is a collection of sixty-six poems, each one corresponding to a book of the Bible. It is available at www.apairofdocspublishing.com.

Helen Prince Hughes Rice, born in Dunn, North Carolina, graduated from Greensboro College in 1945 with a B.A. in Religious Education and a minor in Elementary Education. She and her first husband,

Reverend Miles Preston Hughes, Jr., had six children. She also taught first or second grade for twenty-five years. At forty, Rice received a M.A. from Appalachian State University. Widowed at fifty, she married Wayne Kendall Rice, a chemical engineer. She has nine grandchildren and three great-grandchildren. She resides in Waynesville, North Carolina.

Denise K. Loock is a freelance writer, editor, and speaker. Her devotions and stories appear in best-selling books and magazines. She's also a staff writer for *Journey Christian News*. She's the founder of Dig Deeper Devotions, a website that encourages Christians to dig deeper into the Word of God. Lighthouse Publishing of the Carolinas has released two collections of Loock's devotions—*Open Your Hymnal: Devotions That Harmonize Scripture with Song* (2010) and *Open Your Hymnal Again* (2012). Find out more about these books by visiting www.Amazon.com or www.DigDeeperDevotions.com/books.aspx.

Mary Jo Maples, a native Alabamian, received her undergraduate degree from Mississippi College and her M.A. from Texas A & M University. In addition to the busy life of a pastor's wife, she taught at Blinn Junior College in Bryan, Texas, for six years before joining the faculty at Dallas Baptist University as Assistant Professor of English in 1996. Since her retirement, she has served as an adjunct professor teaching on campus and as of 2007 has served as an online instructor. She's married to Dr. Dick Maples and is the mother of two grown children, eight grandchildren and two great-grandchildren.

Maureen Miller enjoys life with her childhood-sweetheart-turned-husband and their three children on their western North Carolina farm. Together they grow things year round in their greenhouse, gather eggs laid by their chickens, laugh at the antics of goats, horses, and dogs, and give God praise for His goodness. Maureen enjoys reading and writing, as well as serving in youth and women's ministry as a Bible teacher and mentor. When she's not speaking, she's often heard singing God's praise.

Ron Miller retired from the Department of State Foreign Service after thirty-five years. He has lived in, worked in, or visited at least eighty countries. He also held State Department posts in the USA. Ron holds a Bachelor's degree from the University of Maryland and is an Air Force veteran. He's active in the Maggie Valley United Methodist Church. He's also a Christian songwriter, runner, hiker, avid reader, and self-described "news junkie." Ron and his wife, Janette, live in Maggie Valley and have two grown children.

Beth Pleming discovered both an interest in journalism and a love for the mountains at a small college in Colorado. She moved to Maggie Valley in 2006 to pursue a career as a journalist. Her articles have appeared in many news publications in the Carolinas and in Colorado, including *South Carolina Wildlife* and *The South Carolina Encyclopedia*. She served as a crime reporter for Haywood County's newspaper, *The Mountaineer*, for more than six years before launching a career in publishing. The fact that God speaks to us is one of her favorite attributes of His character.

Erlinda Rogers has lived in Waynesville, North Carolina, for the last twelve years. She and her late husband moved from California after his retirement from the Marine Corps. She has two adult sons, Manuel and Anthony, and three grandchildren. She lives with her cat Lucy Luz. She's always enjoyed story time and has written articles for the church she attended in California. This skill has been put on the back burner of her life for a while, but she's now bringing it forth as part of her spiritual renewal.

Anne Catherine Serota Scott is a retired social worker, family therapist, NPO administrator, Christmas tree grower, and nurserywoman. She earned her Doctorate of Ministry at age 55 and serves at Congregation Beth Shiloh Messianic Jewish Synagogue in Asheville, North Carolina. Catherine is single with no children. She is studying Biblical and Modern Hebrew with the goal of serving Messianic congregations in Israel.

Dee Shaw, a former high school science teacher, has always been interested in the physical, educational, and spiritual development of teens. She received the Service to Youth Award from the YMCA and an Outstanding Achievement Award in the Deep River Books 2012 Writer's Contest. She has been a hospital dietitian and Bible study teacher. Her husband and she have served as the pastoral care couple to 600 missionaries of the Presbyterian Church in America and have visited sixty-eight countries. Dee is the mother of three grown children. She and her husband live in North Carolina.

Nathan Tracy is the author of three published books; four other manuscripts are in the final editing stage. Three of his books deal with yachting in a marine setting; the other three are set in the mountains. Tracy was born in Florida but raised in New Hampshire. He worked as a marine insurance adjustor for forty years in Florida, but now lives on the North Carolina side of the Smoky Mountains. Tracy was profoundly saved on a storm-swept beach in Indian Rocks Beach, Florida. Ordained under the ministry of Derek Prince, he has shepherded home groups and co-pastored a church.

Carolyn Underwood, a non-stop work in progress, is joyfully in love with her Lord and Savior Jesus Christ. Serving Him as a teacher for several decades, she is blessed with outrageous adventures only God can design. Married with Ed for thirty-four years, Carolyn has published songs, a short story, readers' theaters, as well as magazine and newspaper articles. She has also sold some of her photography. Quilting and writing vie for her time when she's not playing with her dogs.

Chris Yavelow, author and composer, has received dozens of writing and music awards, both secular and Christian; for example, The Computer Press Association Award for his *Music and Sound Bible*, the *Grand Prix à l'Unanimitè* from the *Rencontres Internationales du Chant Choral* for his *Dona Nobis Pacem*, and commissions from the National Endowment for the Arts for his opera, *The Passion of Vincent van Gogh*, and the National Institute of Music Theater for his opera, *Countdown*. His books have been published by IDG Worldwide, Random House, and Bantam. He lives in Asheville, North Carolina.

www.ingramcontent.com/pod-product-compliance
Lightning Source LLC
Chambersburg PA
CBHW031538040426
42445CB00010B/589